# Try Not To ♥

# LAUGH

**Cupid Endorsed**

# Joke Book

# Challenge

Kevin Clark

## Valentine's ♥ Day Edition

First Printing, 2019

ISBN 9781794038363

# Try Not To Laugh Game Rules

### *Easy Version*

1. Find an opponent or split up into two teams.
2. Team 1 reads a joke to Team 2 from anywhere in the book.
3. The person reading the joke looks right at the opposing person or team and can use silly voices and funny faces if they wish.
4. If Team 2:

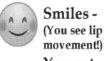 Smiles -
(You see lip movement!)
You get
1 point

 Grins -
(You see teeth!)
You get
2 points

 Laughs -
(You hear noise!)
You get
3 points

5. Read one joke at at time, then switch the giving and receiving teams.
6. The team with most points after five rounds wins! Use the score sheets on the following pages.

### *Challenge Version*

1. Same rules apply except you get one point if you can make the other team laugh. No points for smiling or grinning.

### *Good luck and try not to laugh!*

# SCORE SHEET

|         | TEAM 1 | TEAM 2 |
|---------|--------|--------|
| ROUND 1 |        |        |
| ROUND 2 |        |        |
| ROUND 3 |        |        |
| ROUND 4 |        |        |
| ROUND 5 |        |        |
| TOTAL   |        |        |

|         | TEAM 1 | TEAM 2 |
|---------|--------|--------|
| ROUND 1 |        |        |
| ROUND 2 |        |        |
| ROUND 3 |        |        |
| ROUND 4 |        |        |
| ROUND 5 |        |        |
| TOTAL   |        |        |

|         | TEAM 1 | TEAM 2 |
|---------|--------|--------|
| ROUND 1 |        |        |
| ROUND 2 |        |        |
| ROUND 3 |        |        |
| ROUND 4 |        |        |
| ROUND 5 |        |        |
| TOTAL   |        |        |

|         | TEAM 1 | TEAM 2 |
|---------|--------|--------|
| ROUND 1 |        |        |
| ROUND 2 |        |        |
| ROUND 3 |        |        |
| ROUND 4 |        |        |
| ROUND 5 |        |        |
| TOTAL   |        |        |

|         | TEAM 1 | TEAM 2 |
|---------|--------|--------|
| ROUND 1 |        |        |
| ROUND 2 |        |        |
| ROUND 3 |        |        |
| ROUND 4 |        |        |
| ROUND 5 |        |        |
| TOTAL   |        |        |

|         | TEAM 1 | TEAM 2 |
|---------|--------|--------|
| ROUND 1 |        |        |
| ROUND 2 |        |        |
| ROUND 3 |        |        |
| ROUND 4 |        |        |
| ROUND 5 |        |        |
| TOTAL   |        |        |

|         | TEAM 1 | TEAM 2 |
|---------|--------|--------|
| ROUND 1 |        |        |
| ROUND 2 |        |        |
| ROUND 3 |        |        |
| ROUND 4 |        |        |
| ROUND 5 |        |        |
| TOTAL   |        |        |

|         | TEAM 1 | TEAM 2 |
|---------|--------|--------|
| ROUND 1 |        |        |
| ROUND 2 |        |        |
| ROUND 3 |        |        |
| ROUND 4 |        |        |
| ROUND 5 |        |        |
| TOTAL   |        |        |

# SCORE SHEET

|  | TEAM 1 | TEAM 2 |
|---|---|---|
| ROUND 1 |  |  |
| ROUND 2 |  |  |
| ROUND 3 |  |  |
| ROUND 4 |  |  |
| ROUND 5 |  |  |
| TOTAL |  |  |

|  | TEAM 1 | TEAM 2 |
|---|---|---|
| ROUND 1 |  |  |
| ROUND 2 |  |  |
| ROUND 3 |  |  |
| ROUND 4 |  |  |
| ROUND 5 |  |  |
| TOTAL |  |  |

|  | TEAM 1 | TEAM 2 |
|---|---|---|
| ROUND 1 |  |  |
| ROUND 2 |  |  |
| ROUND 3 |  |  |
| ROUND 4 |  |  |
| ROUND 5 |  |  |
| TOTAL |  |  |

|  | TEAM 1 | TEAM 2 |
|---|---|---|
| ROUND 1 |  |  |
| ROUND 2 |  |  |
| ROUND 3 |  |  |
| ROUND 4 |  |  |
| ROUND 5 |  |  |
| TOTAL |  |  |

|  | TEAM 1 | TEAM 2 |
|---|---|---|
| ROUND 1 |  |  |
| ROUND 2 |  |  |
| ROUND 3 |  |  |
| ROUND 4 |  |  |
| ROUND 5 |  |  |
| TOTAL |  |  |

|  | TEAM 1 | TEAM 2 |
|---|---|---|
| ROUND 1 |  |  |
| ROUND 2 |  |  |
| ROUND 3 |  |  |
| ROUND 4 |  |  |
| ROUND 5 |  |  |
| TOTAL |  |  |

|  | TEAM 1 | TEAM 2 |
|---|---|---|
| ROUND 1 |  |  |
| ROUND 2 |  |  |
| ROUND 3 |  |  |
| ROUND 4 |  |  |
| ROUND 5 |  |  |
| TOTAL |  |  |

|  | TEAM 1 | TEAM 2 |
|---|---|---|
| ROUND 1 |  |  |
| ROUND 2 |  |  |
| ROUND 3 |  |  |
| ROUND 4 |  |  |
| ROUND 5 |  |  |
| TOTAL |  |  |

# SCORE SHEET

|  | TEAM 1 | TEAM 2 |
|---|---|---|
| ROUND 1 |  |  |
| ROUND 2 |  |  |
| ROUND 3 |  |  |
| ROUND 4 |  |  |
| ROUND 5 |  |  |
| TOTAL |  |  |

|  | TEAM 1 | TEAM 2 |
|---|---|---|
| ROUND 1 |  |  |
| ROUND 2 |  |  |
| ROUND 3 |  |  |
| ROUND 4 |  |  |
| ROUND 5 |  |  |
| TOTAL |  |  |

|  | TEAM 1 | TEAM 2 |
|---|---|---|
| ROUND 1 |  |  |
| ROUND 2 |  |  |
| ROUND 3 |  |  |
| ROUND 4 |  |  |
| ROUND 5 |  |  |
| TOTAL |  |  |

|  | TEAM 1 | TEAM 2 |
|---|---|---|
| ROUND 1 |  |  |
| ROUND 2 |  |  |
| ROUND 3 |  |  |
| ROUND 4 |  |  |
| ROUND 5 |  |  |
| TOTAL |  |  |

|  | TEAM 1 | TEAM 2 |
|---|---|---|
| ROUND 1 |  |  |
| ROUND 2 |  |  |
| ROUND 3 |  |  |
| ROUND 4 |  |  |
| ROUND 5 |  |  |
| TOTAL |  |  |

|  | TEAM 1 | TEAM 2 |
|---|---|---|
| ROUND 1 |  |  |
| ROUND 2 |  |  |
| ROUND 3 |  |  |
| ROUND 4 |  |  |
| ROUND 5 |  |  |
| TOTAL |  |  |

|  | TEAM 1 | TEAM 2 |
|---|---|---|
| ROUND 1 |  |  |
| ROUND 2 |  |  |
| ROUND 3 |  |  |
| ROUND 4 |  |  |
| ROUND 5 |  |  |
| TOTAL |  |  |

|  | TEAM 1 | TEAM 2 |
|---|---|---|
| ROUND 1 |  |  |
| ROUND 2 |  |  |
| ROUND 3 |  |  |
| ROUND 4 |  |  |
| ROUND 5 |  |  |
| TOTAL |  |  |

# SCORE SHEET

|  | TEAM 1 | TEAM 2 |
|---|---|---|
| ROUND 1 |  |  |
| ROUND 2 |  |  |
| ROUND 3 |  |  |
| ROUND 4 |  |  |
| ROUND 5 |  |  |
| TOTAL |  |  |

|  | TEAM 1 | TEAM 2 |
|---|---|---|
| ROUND 1 |  |  |
| ROUND 2 |  |  |
| ROUND 3 |  |  |
| ROUND 4 |  |  |
| ROUND 5 |  |  |
| TOTAL |  |  |

|  | TEAM 1 | TEAM 2 |
|---|---|---|
| ROUND 1 |  |  |
| ROUND 2 |  |  |
| ROUND 3 |  |  |
| ROUND 4 |  |  |
| ROUND 5 |  |  |
| TOTAL |  |  |

|  | TEAM 1 | TEAM 2 |
|---|---|---|
| ROUND 1 |  |  |
| ROUND 2 |  |  |
| ROUND 3 |  |  |
| ROUND 4 |  |  |
| ROUND 5 |  |  |
| TOTAL |  |  |

|  | TEAM 1 | TEAM 2 |
|---|---|---|
| ROUND 1 |  |  |
| ROUND 2 |  |  |
| ROUND 3 |  |  |
| ROUND 4 |  |  |
| ROUND 5 |  |  |
| TOTAL |  |  |

|  | TEAM 1 | TEAM 2 |
|---|---|---|
| ROUND 1 |  |  |
| ROUND 2 |  |  |
| ROUND 3 |  |  |
| ROUND 4 |  |  |
| ROUND 5 |  |  |
| TOTAL |  |  |

|  | TEAM 1 | TEAM 2 |
|---|---|---|
| ROUND 1 |  |  |
| ROUND 2 |  |  |
| ROUND 3 |  |  |
| ROUND 4 |  |  |
| ROUND 5 |  |  |
| TOTAL |  |  |

|  | TEAM 1 | TEAM 2 |
|---|---|---|
| ROUND 1 |  |  |
| ROUND 2 |  |  |
| ROUND 3 |  |  |
| ROUND 4 |  |  |
| ROUND 5 |  |  |
| TOTAL |  |  |

What happens when two single buffalo meet up, fall in love and run away to get married?

They buffalope!

What did the French chef give his wife for Valentine's Day?

A hug and a quiche.

What do you call a very small valentine?

A valen-tiny!

What did the pickle say to his Valentine?

"You mean a great *dill* to me."

What did one volcano say to the other
on Valentine's Day?

I lava you.

Why did the two knives go to the dance
together?

Because they both looked sharp!

What does someone who loves their car
do on February 14th?

They give it a valen-shine!

What do you call a fruit that's in love?

Peachy-Keen

What is the best thing to put on
Valentine's Day chocolate?

Your teeth.

What did the rabbit say to his girlfriend on Valentine's Day?

"Some bunny wuvs you!"

Knock Knock.
Who's there?
Pauline!
Pauline Who?
I think I'm Pauline in love with you.

Did you hear about the two centipedes in love?

They would complete each others centi-ses.

What candy is only for girls?

HER-SHEy's Kisses.

What do you call lettuce that's in love?

Head over heels.

What kind of fruit do calendars love?

Dates!

What did the whale say to his girlfriend on Valentine's Day?

"Whale you be mine?"

What did one beet say to the other on Valentine's Day?

"You make my heart beet faster!"

Happy
Valentine's
Day

What happened when the magicians went on a date?

It was love at first slight.

What do cars do at the Valentine's Day party?

Brake dance

What's the best thing about Valentine's Day?

The day after when all the chocolate goes on sale!

Why didn't the skeleton break up with his girlfriend on Valentine's Day?

He didn't have the heart!

What do squirrels give for Valentine's Day?

Forget-me-nuts.

Why did the woman fall in love with the trapeze artist?

Because of his net worth.

What kind of flowers should you never give on Valentine's Day?

Cauliflowers.

Why do zombies only date intelligent women?

They just love a woman with BRAAAINS!

Knock Knock.
Who's there?
Rome!
Rome who?
Rome is where the heart is!

What do Valentine's Day flowers call their best friends?

Buds.

Why do melons have to get married in churches?

Because they cantaloupe!

Why do oars fall in love?

Because they're row-mantic.

Happy Valentine's Day!

What food is crazy about Valentine's Day chocolates?

A cocoa-nut.

What did Frankenstein say to his girlfriend on Valentine's Day?

Be my Valen-stein!

Why did the two shoemakers got married?

Because they were sole mates.

Knock Knock!
Who's There?
Amal!
Amal Who?
I'm in love, Amal shook up!

What did Pilgrims give each other on Valentine's Day?

Mayflowers.

What happened when the woman stole the policeman's heart?

He did a cardiac arrest.

Two antennae met on a roof, fell in love and got married.
Their wedding ceremony wasn't fancy.
The reception, however, was excellent!

How did the telephone propose to his girlfriend?

He gave her a ring.

What did the painter say to her boyfriend?

"I love you with all my art!"

What did the husband get his wife on Valentine's Day to take her breath away?

A treadmill.

What did the Mr. Mentos say to Mrs. Mentos?

"It's Valentine's Day and we're mint for each other."

What did the man with the broken leg say to his nurse?

"I've got a crutch on you!"

Did you hear about the nearsighted porcupine?

He fell in love with a pincushion!

Where does spaghetti go on Valentine's
Day?

The meat ball!

What did the paper clip say to the
magnet?

"I find you super attractive!"

What is an astronaut's favorite
chocolate?

A Milky Way!

What is the opposite of Chocolate?

Choco-early.

What do you get when you dip a kitten in chocolate?

A Kitty Kat bar!

What did the boy bear say to the girl bear on Valentine's Day?

"I love you beary much!"

Why is Valentine's Day the best day for a celebration?

Because you can really party hearty!

What did the recently reunited girlfriend say to her boyfriend on a foggy Valentine's Day?

"I mist you."

Why did the computer fall in love with the Wi-Fi?

They just had a connection.

Knock Knock!
Who's there?
Juno!
Juno who?
Juno I love you, right?

What did the boy sheep say to the girl
sheep on Valentine's Day?

"I love ewe."

What did the girl sheep say to the boy
sheep on Valentine's Day?

"Hey, you're not so baaaa-d yourself!"

Did you hear what happened after Mr. Goodbar and Peppermint Patty got married?

They had a baby, Ruth.

What is an alien's favorite chocolate?

A Mars bar!

What happened when two vampires went on a blind date?

It was love at first bite!

What happened to the price of flowers on Valentine's Day?

They rose to the occasion.

## Love
## Love
## Love

A boy finds a frog that says, "Kiss me and I will become a beautiful princess." The boy looks at the frog and puts it in his pocket. "Hey," the frog says, "don't you want me to turn into a princess?" "Nah," the boy says, "I'd rather have a talking frog."

What did Batman give Catwoman on Valentine's Day?

A mouse.

Why couldn't the skeleton dance at the Valentine's Day party?

Because he had no body to dance with!

What kind of chocolate do they sell at the airport?

Plane Chocolate!

Knock Knock!
Who's There?
Kenya!
Kenya who?
"Kenya feel the love tonight?"

What did one flame say to the other on Valentine's Day?

"We're a perfect match."

Why did the man send his wife's Valentine through Twitter?

Because she is his tweetheart.

Why are veins so sensitive about blood?

They take it to heart.

What did one calculator say to the other on Valentine's Day?

"How do I love thee? Let me count the ways."

Happy Valentines Day

Man: I really love hotels.

Woman: If you love them so much, why don't you Marriott?!

What does a chocolate bar do when it hears a good joke?

It Snickers.

What happens when you fall in love with a French chef?

You get buttered up.

What happened to the oyster at the Valentine's Day dance?

It pulled a mussel!

Did you hear about the man who promised his girlfriend a diamond for Valentine's Day?

He took her to a baseball game.

What was the French cat's favorite Valentine's Day dessert?

Chocolate mousse

What do you call two birds in love?

Tweethearts.

What did the light bulb say to his wife?

"I love you watts and watts!"

Why did the boy put a candy bar under his pillow?

So he would have sweet dreams!

Why did the girl put clothes on the Valentine's Day card she was sending?

She thought it needed to be ad-dressed.

What do you call a sheep covered in chocolate?

A Hershey baaaaa.

What is the most romantic city in England?

Loverpool.

What did the ghost call his sweetheart?

His goul-friend.

Knock, knock.
Who's There?
Alec.
Alec Who?
Alec to kiss you on the cheek!

What did one piece of string say to the other on February 14th?

"Be my valen-twine."

What did the valentine say to the stamp?

"Stick with me, and we'll go places!"

What did the M&M go to college?

Because he wanted to be a Smarty.

Knock Knock!
Who's there?
Frank.
Frank Who?
Frank you for being my Valentine.

Where do fortune tellers dance on
Valentine's Day?

At the crystal ball.

What did the farmer give his wife for
Valentine's Day?

Hogs and kisses.

Did you hear about the snake love letter?

He sealed it with a hiss.

What did the circle say to the triangle on Valentine's Day?

I think you're acute.

What does a carpet salesman give his wife for Valentine's Day?

Rugs and kisses.

What did the boy octopus say to the girl octopus?

"I wann hold your hand, hand, hand, hand, hand, hand, hand, hand."

What did cavemen give their wives on Valentine's Day?

Lots of "ughs" and kisses.

What did the blueberry say to his wife on Valentine's Day?

"I love you berry much."

What did the man call his wife who gave him a wallet made of soft leather?

His suede heart.

What do you get when you cross a dog with a valentine card?

A card that says "I love you, drool-ly. Drool-ly, I do!"

What did the lamp say to the switch?

"You turn me on."

What did one muffin say to the other on Valentine' Day?

You're my stud muffin!

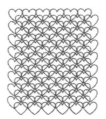

What is a ram's favorite saying on February 14th?

I only have eyes for ewe, deer.

Why do skunks celebrate Valentine's Day?

Because they're scent-imental.

What did the girl cat say to the boy cat
on Valentine's Day?

"You're purrr-fect for me."

Why do magicians love chocolate?

Because they perform a lot of Twix.

What happened when the two tennis
players met?

It was lob at first sight.

# Tongue Twisters!

*Make your opponent say a tongue twister five times fast.*
*If they start laughing, they lose!*

Cathy caught Candace counting all the candy.

Ann and Andy's anniversary is in April.

Four furious friends fought for the flowers.

I thought, I thought of thinking of thanking you.

Mister Kister treat so sweet,
Mister Kister when can I eat?

Love's a feeling you feel when you feel you're going to feel the feeling you've never felt before.

She sees chocolate cheese.

There was a minimum of cinnamon in
the aluminum pan.

If you can can candy,
how many candies can a candy canner
can
if he can can candy cans?

Addy adores Aidan and Arnold.

Sheena leads, Sheila needs.

Rolling red wagons.

Mommy made me eat my M&Ms.

I know a boy named Tate
who dined with his girl at eight.
I'm unable to state what Tate ate at
eight
or what Tate's date ate at eight.

The bottle of perfume that Willy sent
was highly displeasing to Millicent.


I thought a thought.
But the thought I thought
Wasn't the thought I thought I thought.


Meter maid Mary married manly
Matthew Marcus Mayo,
a moody male mailman moving mostly
metered mail.


The king would sing, about a ring that
would go ding ding ding.


Moses supposes his toeses are roses.
But Moses supposes wrong.


Courtney Ship was in a courtship on a
corky ship.


Freddy is ready to roast red roses.
Ready for Freddy's roasted red roses?

Susie sits shining her sweetheart's sweets.

A synonym for cinnamon is a cinnamon synonym.

Nope, an antelope can't elope with a cantaloupe.

Sheila snapped a selfie with Sophie's silver cell phone.

A happy hippo hugged and hiccupped.

Made in the USA
San Bernardino, CA
09 February 2019